It is Hidden

Written by Paul Harrison

Collins

Look for it.

The toad is hidden at the bottom.

Can you see it?

The lizard is high up.

Look for it.

This looper moth is on the bark.

Can you see it?

The shark is by the reef.

Look for it.

The big cat is hard to see.

Can you see it?

This night owl is hidden.

Did you see?

 After reading

Letters and Sounds: Phase 3

Word count: 61

Focus phonemes: /ee/ /oo/ /or/ /oa/ /ar/ /igh/ /oo/ /er/ /ow/, dd, tt

Common exception words: you, by, the, to

Curriculum links: Understanding the world: The world

Early learning goals: Listening and attention: children listen attentively in a range of situations; Understanding: answer 'how' and 'why' questions about their experiences and in response to stories or events; Reading: read and understand simple sentences, use phonic knowledge to decode regular words and read them aloud accurately, read some common irregular words

Developing fluency

- Your child may enjoy hearing you read the book.
- You could take turns to read a page. Model reading with lots of expression and encourage your child to do the same.

Phonic practice

- Practise reading words with long vowel sounds together. Look at the word **toad**. Ask your child to sound talk and blend the letter sounds t/oa/d.
- Do the same with the following words:

  h/igh high   sh/ar/k shark   r/ee/f reef   h/ar/d hard

Extending vocabulary

- Ask your child if they can tell you the opposite of each of the following words (opposites/antonyms):

  night (day)

  high (low)

  on (off)

  bottom (top)